CLASSIC LITERATURE BOOKS

The Sorrows Of Belgium
A Play In Six Scenes

Leonid Andreyev

Translated by
Herman Bernstein

Table of Contents

CHARACTERS

Count Clairmont.
Emil Grelieu—A Famous Belgian Author.
Jeanne—His Wife.
Pierre } Their sons.
Maurice}
Lagard—Member of the Cabinet.
General—Adjutant to Count Clairmont.
Insane Girl.
François—Gardener.
Henrietta } Grelieu's Servants.
Silvina }
Commander of the German Armies in Belgium.
Von Blumenfeld.
Von Ritzau }
Von Stein } Officers.
Von Schauss}
Kloetz—Military Engineer.
Zigler—Telegraphist.
Greitzer.
German Officer.
Belgian Peasant.
Doctor Langloi.
A Chauffeur—A Belgian.

SCENE I

The action takes place in Belgium, at the beginning of the war of 1914. The scene represents a garden near the villa of the famous Belgian author, Emil Grelieu. Beyond the tops of low trees, beyond the stone fence which divides Grelieu's estate from the neighboring gardens, are seen the outlines of the red roofs of the houses in the small town, of the Town Hall, and of an ancient church. There the people already know about the war; there the church bells are ringing uneasily, while in the garden there is still peace. A small, splendidly kept flower garden; beautiful and fragrant flowers; shrubbery in bloom; a nook of a hothouse. The glass covers are half open. The sun is shining softly; there is in the air the bluish mist of a warm and quiet day, and all colors seem tenderly soft; only in the foreground the colors of the flowers stand out in sharp relief.

François is sitting and clipping roses at one of the flower beds. He is an old and deaf, stern Belgian, with long, gray hair. He holds in his mouth an earthen pipe. François is working. He does not hear the tolling of the bells. He is alone in the garden, and it seems to him that all is calm and quiet.

But something fills him with faint alarm. He hears an indistinct call. He looks around—but sees no one. He hums to himself a song without words. Suddenly he stops, straightens himself, holding the scissors in his hands, and looks around again.
FRANÇOIS

Who has called me?

He sees no one. He looks at the hothouse—it seems to him that some one is calling him from there.

I hear you, Monsieur Emil, I am here.

He sees no one. He frowns and cries angrily.

Who is calling me? No one here.

He looks at the sky, then at the flowers, and resumes his work quietly.

They say I am deaf. But I heard some one calling me twice: "François!" "François!" No, perhaps it is my blood, making a noise in my ears.

Silence. But his uneasiness does not subside; he listens again.

I can still hear some one calling me: "François!"

Very well; here is François, and if anyone needs me he may call me again. I shall not run. I can't hear the chirping of the birds; the birds have long since become silent for me. What nonsense—these birds! Very well, I am deaf—does anyone think I am going to cry over it?

Twitches his mouth into a smile.

And my eyes? That is another matter. My eyes! Why are you forever silent, François? Why should I speak if I do not hear your foolish answer? It is all nonsense—to talk and to listen. I can see more than you can hear.

Laughs.

Yes, I see this. This does not talk either, but bend down to it and you will learn more than Solomon ever knew. That is what the Bible says—Solomon. To you the earth is noise and prattle, while to me it is like a Madonna in colors upon a picture. Like a Madonna in colors.

The bell is ringing. In the distance a youthful voice calls "Papa!" "Papa!" Then, "François!" Maurice, Emil Grelieu's younger son, a youth of about 17, appears, coming quickly from the house. He calls François once more, but François does not hear. Finally he shouts right next to his ear.

MAURICE

François, what is the matter with you? I am calling you. I am calling you. Haven't you seen papa?

FRANÇOIS

Calmly, without turning around.

Did you call me, Maurice? I heard your call long ago.

MAURICE

You heard me, but did not respond. How obstinate you are! Haven't you seen papa? I am looking for him everywhere. Quick! Where is papa?

FRANÇOIS

Papa?

MAURICE

Shouts.

Where is papa? Haven't you seen him? Silvina says he went to the hothouse. Do you hear?

FRANÇOIS

He is not there. I spoke to Monsieur this morning, but since then I have not seen him. No.

MAURICE

What is to be done? How they are tolling! François, what is to be done—do you hear them tolling?

FRANÇOIS

Ah! I hear. Will you take some roses, my boy?

MAURICE

You don't understand anything—you are beyond endurance! They are running in the streets, they are all running there, and papa is not here. I will run over there, too, at once. Perhaps he is there. What a day!

FRANÇOIS

Who is running?

MAURICE

You don't understand anything!

Shouts.

They have entered Belgium!
FRANÇOIS
Who has entered Belgium?
MAURICE
They—the Prussians. Can't you understand? It's war! War! Imagine what will happen. Pierre will have to go, and so will I go. I will not stay here under any circumstances.
FRANÇOIS
Straightening himself, dropping the scissors.
War? What nonsense, my boy! Who has entered Belgium?
MAURICE
They—the Prussians. Pierre will go now, and I will go—I will not stay away under any circumstances, understand? What will become of Belgium now?—it is hard to conceive it. They entered Belgium yesterday—do you understand—what scoundrels!
In the distance, along the narrow streets of the town, an uneasy sound of footsteps and wheels is growing rapidly. Distinct voices and outcries blend into a dull, suppressed, ominous noise, full of alarm. The tolling, as though tired, now subsides, now turns almost to a shriek. François tries vainly to hear something. Then he takes up the scissors again angrily.
MAURICE
François!
FRANÇOIS
Sternly.
That's all nonsense! What are you prating, my boy? There is no war—that is impossible.
MAURICE
You are a foolish old man, yourself! They have entered Belgium—do you understand—they are here already.
FRANÇOIS
That's not true.
MAURICE
Why isn't it true?
FRANÇOIS
Because that is impossible. The newspapers print nonsense, and they have all gone mad. Fools, and nothing more— madmen. What Prussians? Young man, you have no right to make sport of me like this.
MAURICE
But listen—
FRANÇOIS
Prussians! What Prussians? I don't know any Prussians, and I don't want to know them.
MAURICE
But understand, old man, they are already bombarding Liège!

FRANÇOIS

No!

MAURICE

They have killed many people. What a strange man you are! Don't you hear the tolling of the bells? The people are on the square. They are all running. The women are crying. What is that?

FRANÇOIS

Angrily.

You are stepping on the flower bed. Get off!

MAURICE

Don't bother me! Why are they shouting so loudly? Something has happened there. The sound of a trumpet is heard in the distance. The shouting of the crowd is growing ever louder. Sounds of the Belgian hymn are heard faintly. Suddenly an ominous silence follows the noise, and then the lone sound of the tolling bells.

MAURICE

Now they are quiet.... What does it mean?

FRANÇOIS

Nonsense, nonsense!

Infuriated.

You are stepping on the flower bed again. Get off! You have all lost your reason! Go, go! The Prussians!...

MAURICE

You have lost your reason!

FRANÇOIS

I am seventy years old, and you tell me about the Prussians. Go!

Again the shouting of the crowd is heard. Silvina, the chambermaid, runs out of the house and calls: "Monsieur Maurice!"

SILVINA

Please, come into the house. Madame Jeanne is calling you. Madame is going away. Please, come.

MAURICE

And papa?

SILVINA

He isn't here yet. Come!

Both move away. François sits down at the flower bed impatiently.

MAURICE

You don't understand, Silvina. He does not believe that there is a war.

SILVINA

It is very dreadful, Monsieur Maurice. I am afraid—

They go out. François looks after them angrily, adjusts his apron, and prepares to resume his work.

FRANÇOIS

Madmen! I am seventy years old. I am seventy years old, and they want me to believe a story about Prussians. Nonsense, they are crazy! Prussians! But it is true that I don't hear anything.

Rising, he listens attentively.

No, not a sound. Or do I hear something? Oh, the devil take it! I can't hear a sound. Impossible! No, no, impossible! But what is that? How could I believe that in this calm sky—in this calm sky—

The din of battle is growing. François listens again and hears it. He grows thoughtful. His eyes express fright. He looks as though he had suddenly solved a terrible problem. He moves to and fro, his head bent down, as though trying to catch the sounds. Suddenly he throws down the scissors. He is seized with a feeling of terror. He raises his hands.

I hear it. No. No. Now I don't hear a sound. Oh, God, give me the power to hear!

He tries again to catch the fleeting sounds, his head bent, his neck outstretched. His hair is disheveled. His eyes stare. Suddenly, by a great effort, he hears the tolling of the bells and voices full of despair. He retreats and raises his hands again.

My God! They are tolling! They are crying! War! What war? What war? Eh, who is there—who is shouting "War!"?

The sound of the bells and the cries grows louder. Emil Grelieu appears, walking quickly in the alley.

EMIL GRELIEU

What are you shouting, François? Where is Maurice? No one is in the house.

FRANÇOIS

Is it war?

EMIL GRELIEU

Yes, yes, it is war. The Prussians have entered Belgium. But you don't hear anything.

FRANÇOIS

Painfully trying to catch the sounds.

I hear, I hear; are they killing?

EMIL GRELIEU

Yes, they are killing. The Prussians have entered Belgium. Where is Maurice?

FRANÇOIS

But, Monsieur Emil—but, Monsieur, what Prussians? Pardon me; I am seventy years old, and I lost my sense of hearing long ago.

Weeps.

Is it really a war?

EMIL GRELIEU

Yes, it is a real war. I can't understand it either. But the fighting has already commenced. I can't realize it myself, but it is war, old man.

FRANÇOIS

Tell me, Monsieur. Tell me about it. I believe you as I believe God. Tell me. I can hear you. Are they killing?

EMIL GRELIEU

It is war! What horror, François. It is very hard to understand it—yes, very hard. Frowns and rubs his high, pale forehead nervously.

FRANÇOIS

Bent, weeps, his head shaking.

And the flowers? Our flowers?

EMIL GRELIEU

Absentmindedly.

Our flowers? Don't cry, François—ah, what is that?

The tolling of the bells subsides. The crying and the shouting of the crowd changes, into a harmonious volume of sound—somebody is hailed in the distance. An important announcement seems to have been made there.

EMIL GRELIEU

Absentmindedly.

Our people are expecting the King there—he is on his way to Liège! Yes, yes— Silence. Suddenly there is a sound like the crash of thunder. Then it changes into a song—the crowd is singing the Belgian hymn.

Curtain

SCENE II

The reception hall in Emil Grelieu's villa. Plenty of air, light, and flowers. Large, windows overlooking the garden in bloom. One small window is almost entirely covered with the leaves of vines.

In the room are Emil Grelieu and his elder son, Pierre, a handsome, pale, and frail-looking young man. He is dressed in military uniform. They pace up and down the room slowly. It is evident that Pierre is anxious to walk faster, but out of respect for his father he slackens his pace.

EMIL GRELIEU

How many kilometers?

PIERRE

Twenty-five or thirty kilometers to Tirlemont—and here—

EMIL GRELIEU

Seventy-four or five—

PIERRE

Seventy-five—yes, about a hundred kilometers. It's not far, father.

EMIL GRELIEU

Not far. It seemed to me that I heard cannonading. I heard it last night.

PIERRE

No, it's hardly possible.

EMIL GRELIEU

Yes, I was mistaken. But the rays of the searchlights could be seen. They must be very powerful searchlights. Mamma saw them too.

PIERRE

Really? You are suffering from insomnia again, father?

EMIL GRELIEU

I sleep well. A hundred kilometers—a hundred kilometers—

Silence. Pierre looks at his father attentively.

PIERRE

Father!

EMIL GRELIEU

Well? It's too early for you, Pierre—you have three hours yet before your train starts. I am watching the time.

PIERRE

I know, father. No, I am thinking of something else—. Father, tell me, have you still any hopes?

Silence.

I am hesitating, I feel somewhat embarrassed to speak to you—you are so much wiser, so far above me, father.... Yes, yes, it's nonsense, of course, but that which I have learned in the army during these days gives me very little hope. They are coming in such a compact mass of people, of iron, machines, arms and horses, that there is no possibility of stopping them. It seems to me that seismographs must indicate the place over which they pass—they press the ground with such force. And we are so few in number!

EMIL GRELIEU

Yes, we are very few in number.

PIERRE

Very, very few, father! Dreadfully few! Even if we were invulnerable and deathless, even if we kept killing them off day and night, day and night, we would drop from fatigue and exhaustion before we stopped them. But we are mortal—and they have terrible guns, father! You are silent? You are thinking of our Maurice—I have caused you pain?

EMIL GRELIEU

There is little of the human in their movements. Do not think of Maurice—he will live. A human being has a face, Pierre. Every human being has his own face, but they have no faces. When I try to picture them to myself, I see only the lights, projectors, automobiles—those terrible guns—and something walking, walking. And those vulgar mustaches of Wilhelm—but that is a mask, an immobile mask, which has stood over Europe for a quarter of a century—what is behind it? Those vulgar mustaches—and suddenly so much misery, so much bloodshed and destruction! It is a mask!

PIERRE

Almost to himself.

If there were only not so many of them, not so many—. Father, I believe that Maurice will live. He is a lucky boy. But what does mamma think about it?

EMIL GRELIEU

What mamma thinks?

Enter François. Sternly, without looking at anyone, he waters the flowers.

And what does he think? Look at him.

PIERRE

He can hardly hear anything. François!

EMIL GRELIEU

I don't know whether he hears anything or not. But there was a time when he did hear. He is silent, Pierre, and he furiously denies war. He denies it by work—he works alone in the garden as if nothing had happened. Our house is full of refugees. Mamma and everyone else in the house are busy, feeding them, washing the children—mamma is washing them—but he does not seem to notice anything. He denies war! Now he is bursting from anxiety to hear or guess what we are saying, but do you see the expression of his face? If you start to talk to him he will go away.

PIERRE

François!

EMIL GRELIEU

Don't bother him. He wants to be crafty. Perhaps he hears us. You ask me what mother is thinking of. Do I know? Who can tell? You see that she is not here, and yet these are your last hours at home. Yes, in this house—I am speaking of the house. She is young and resolute as ever, she walks just as lightly and is just as clear-headed, but she is not here. She is simply not here, Pierre.

PIERRE

Is she concealing something?

EMIL GRELIEU

No, she is not concealing anything, but she has gone into the depths of her own self, where all is silence and mystery. She is living through her motherhood again, from the very beginning—do you understand? when you and Maurice were not yet born—but in this she is crafty, like François. Sometimes I see clearly that she is suffering unbearably, that she is terrified by the war—. But she smiles in answer and then I see something else—I see how there has suddenly awakened in her the prehistoric woman—the woman who handed her husband the fighting club—. Wait, the soldiers are coming again!

Military music is heard in the distance, nearing.

PIERRE

Yes, according to the assignment, it is the Ninth Regiment.

EMIL GRELIEU

Let us hear it, Pierre. I hear this music several times a day. There it starts on the right, and there it dies down. Always there.

They listen.

But they are brave fellows!

PIERRE

Yes.

Both listen attentively at the window. François looks at them askance and tries in vain to hear. The music begins to die out.

EMIL GRELIEU

Walking away from the window.

Yesterday they played the "Marseillaise." But they are brave fellows!

Emil Grelieu's wife enters quickly.

JEANNE

Do you hear it? How beautiful! Even our refugees smiled when they heard it. Emil, I have brought you some telegrams, here. I have read them.

EMIL GRELIEU

What is it? Let me have them!

Reading the telegrams, he staggers to an armchair and sinks into it. He turns pale.

PIERRE

What is it, father?

EMIL GRELIEU

Read!

Pierre reads it over the shoulder of his father. The woman looks at them with an enigmatical expression upon her face. She sits calmly, her beautiful head thrown back. Emil Grelieu rises quickly, and both he and his son start to pace the room in opposite directions.

PIERRE

Do you see?

EMIL GRELIEU

Yes.

PIERRE

Do you see?

EMIL GRELIEU

Yes! Yes!

JEANNE

As though indifferently.

Emil, was that an interesting library which they have destroyed? I don't know.

EMIL GRELIEU

Yes, very. But what are you asking me, Jeanne? How can you speak?

JEANNE

Oh, I speak only of those books! Tell me, were there many books there?

EMIL GRELIEU

Yes, many, many!

JEANNE

And they've burned them?

She hums softly in afresh, strong voice.

"Only the halo of the arts crowns law, liberty, and the King!—Law—"

EMIL GRELIEU

Books, books.

JEANNE

And there was also a Cathedral there. Oh, I remember it! Isn't it true, Emil, that it was a beautiful structure?

Hums.

"Law, liberty, and the King—"

PIERRE

Father!

What?

EMIL GRELIEU

He walks up and down the room.

JEANNE

Pierre, it will soon be time for you to leave. I'll give you something to eat at once. Pierre, do you think it is true that they are killing women and children? I don't know.

PIERRE

It is true, mother.

EMIL GRELIEU

How can you say it, Jeanne? You don't know?

JEANNE

I say this on account of the children. Yes, there they write that they are killing children, so they write there. And all this was crowded upon that little slip of paper— and the children, as well as the fire—

Rises quickly and walks away, humming.

EMIL GRELIEU

Where are you going, Jeanne?

JEANNE

Nowhere in particular. François, do you hear? They are murdering our women and children. François! François!

Without turning around, François walks out, his shoulders bent. All look after him. Jeanne goes to the other door with a strange half-smile.

PIERRE

Mamma!

JEANNE

I will return directly.

EMIL GRELIEU

What shall I call them? What can I call them? My dear Pierre, my boy, what shall I call them?

PIERRE

You are greatly agitated, father.

EMIL GRELIEU

I have always thought, I have always been convinced that words were at my command, but here I stand before this monstrous, inexplicable—I don't know, I don't know what to call them. My heart is crying out, I hear its voice, but the word! Pierre, you are a student, you are young, your words are direct and pure—Pierre, find the word!

PIERRE

You want me to find it, father? Yes, I was a student, and I knew certain words: Peace, Right, Humanity. But now you see! My heart is crying too, but I do not know what to call these scoundrels. Scoundrels? That is not sufficient.

In despair.

Not sufficient.

EMIL GRELIEU

That is not strong enough. Pierre, I have decided—

PIERRE

Decided?

EMIL GRELIEU

Yes, I am going.

PIERRE

You, father?

EMIL GRELIEU

I decided to do it several days ago—even then, at the very beginning. And I really don't know why I—. Oh, yes, I had to overcome within me—my love for flowers. Ironically.

Yes, Pierre, my love for flowers. Oh, my boy, it is so hard to change from flowers to iron and blood!

PIERRE

Father, I dare not contradict you.

EMIL GRELIEU

No, no, you dare not. It is not necessary. Listen, Pierre, you must examine me as a physician.

PIERRE

I am only a student, father.

EMIL GRELIEU

Yes, but you know enough to say—. You see, Pierre, I must not burden our little army with a single superfluous sick or weak man. Isn't that so? I must bring with me strength and power, not shattered health. Isn't that so? And I am asking you, Pierre, to examine me, simply as a physician, as a young physician. But I feel somewhat embarrassed with you—. Must I take this off, or can you do it without removing this?

PIERRE

It can be done this way.

EMIL GRELIEU

I think so, too. And—must I tell you everything, or—? At any rate, I will tell you that I have not had any serious ailments, and for my years I am a rather strong, healthy man. You know what a life I am leading.

PIERRE

That is unnecessary, father.

EMIL GRELIEU

It is necessary. You are a physician. I want to say that in my life there were none of those unwholesome—and bad excesses. Oh, the devil take it, how hard it is to speak of it.

PIERRE

Papa, I know all this.

Quickly kisses his father's hand. Silence.

EMIL GRELIEU

But it is necessary to take my pulse, Pierre, I beg of you.

PIERRE

Smiling faintly.

It isn't necessary to do even that. As a physician, I can tell you that you are healthy, but—you are unfit for war, you are unfit for war, father! I am listening to you and I feel like crying, father.

EMIL GRELIEU

Thoughtfully.

Yes, yes. But perhaps it is not necessary to cry. Do you think, Pierre, that I should not kill? Pierre, you think, that I, Emil Grelieu, must not kill under any circumstances and at any time?

PIERRE

Softly.

I dare not touch upon your conscience, father.

EMIL GRELIEU

Yes, that is a terrible question for a man. I must kill, Pierre. Of course, I could take your gun, but not to fire—no, that would have been disgusting, a sacrilegious deception! When my humble people are condemned to kill, who am I that I should keep my hands clean? That would be disgusting cleanliness, obnoxious saintliness. My humble nation did not desire to kill, but it was forced, and it has become a murderer. So I, too, must become a murderer, together with my nation. Upon whose shoulders will I place the sin—upon the shoulders of our youths and children? No, Pierre. And if ever the Higher Conscience of the world will call my dear people to the terrible accounting, if it will call you and Maurice, my children, and will say to you: "What have you done? You have murdered!" I will come forward and will say: "First you must judge me; I have also murdered—and you know that I am an honest man!"

Pierre sits motionless, his face covered with his hands. Enter Jeanne, unnoticed.

PIERRE

Uncovering his face.

But you must not die! You have no right!

EMIL GRELIEU

Loudly, and with contempt.

Oh, death!

They notice Jeanne, and grow silent. Jeanne sits down and speaks in the same tone of strange, almost cheerful calm.

JEANNE

Emil, she is here again.

EMIL GRELIEU

Yes? She is here again. Where has she been the last two nights?

JEANNE

She does not know herself. Emil, her dress and her hands were in blood.

EMIL GRELIEU

She is wounded?

JEANNE

No, it is not her own blood, and by the color I could not tell whose blood it is.
PIERRE
Who is that, mother?
JEANNE
A girl. Just a girl. She's insane. I have combed her hair and put a clean dress on her. She has beautiful hair. Emil, I have heard something—I understand that you want to go—?
EMIL GRELIEU
Yes.
JEANNE
Together with your children, Emil?
EMIL GRELIEU
Yes. Pierre has examined me and finds that I am fit to enter the ranks.
JEANNE
You intend to go tomorrow?
EMIL GRELIEU
Yes.
JEANNE
You cannot manage it today. Pierre, you have only an hour and a half left.
Silence.
PIERRE
Mamma! Tell him that he must not—Forgive me, father!—that he should not go. Isn't that true, mother? Tell him! He has given to the nation his two sons—what more should he give? He has no right to give more.
JEANNE
More, Pierre?
PIERRE
Yes,—his life. You love him; you, yourself, would die if he were killed—tell him that, mother!
JEANNE
Yes, I love him. I love you, too.
PIERRE
Oh, what are we, Maurice and I? But he! Just as they have no right to destroy temples in war or to bum libraries, just as they have no right to touch the eternal, so he— he—has no right to die. I am speaking not as your son, no; but to kill Emil Grelieu— that would be worse than to bum books. Listen to me! You have brought me into this world. Listen to me!—although I am young and should be silent—Listen to me! They have already robbed us. They have deprived us of our land and of the air; they have destroyed our treasures which have been created by the genius of our people, and now we would cast our best men into their jaws! What does that mean? What will remain of us? Let them kill us all, let our land be turned into a waste desert, let all

living creatures be burned to death, but as long as he lives, Belgium is alive! What is Belgium without him? Oh, do not be silent, mother! Tell him!

Silence.

EMIL GRELIEU

Somewhat sternly.

Calm yourself, Pierre!

JEANNE

Yesterday I—no, Pierre, that isn't what I was going to say—I don't know anything about it. How could I know? But yesterday I—it is hard to get vegetables, and even bread, here—so I went to town, and for some reason we did not go in that direction, but nearer the field of battle—. How strange it is that we found ourselves there! And there I saw them coming—

EMIL GRELIEU

Whom?

JEANNE

Our soldiers. They were coming from there—where the battle raged for four days. There were not many of them—about a hundred or two hundred. But we all—there were so many people in the streets—we all stepped back to the wall in order to make way for them. Emil, just think of it; how strange! They did not see us, and we would have been in their way! They were black from smoke, from mud, from dried blood, and they were swaying from fatigue. They were all thin—as consumptives. But that is nothing, that is all nothing. Their eyes—what was it, Emil? They did not see their surroundings, they still reflected that which they had seen there—fire and smoke and death—and what else? Some one said: "Here are people returning from hell." We all bowed to them, we bowed to them, but they did not see that either. Is that possible, Emil?

EMIL GRELIEU

Yes, Jeanne, that is possible.

PIERRE

And he will go to that inferno?

Silence. Emil Grelieu walks over to his wife and kisses her hand. She looks at his head with a smile. Suddenly she rises.

JEANNE

Forgive me; there is something else I must say—

She moves quickly and lightly, but suddenly, as though stumbling over an invisible obstacle, falls on one knee. Then she tries to rise, kneels, pale and still smiling, bending to one side. They rush over to her and lift her from the ground.

PIERRE

Mamma! Mamma!

EMIL GRELIEU

You have a headache? Jeanne, my dearest, what ails you?

20

She pushes them aside, stands up firmly, trying to conceal her nervousness.

JEANNE

What is it? What? Don't trouble, Emil! My head? No, no! My foot slipped—you know, the one that pained me. You see, I can walk now.

EMIL GRELIEU

A glass of water, Pierre.

JEANNE

What for? How absurd!

But Pierre had already gone out. Jeanne sits down, hangs her head, as one guilty, endeavoring not to look into his eyes.

JEANNE

What an excitable youth—your Pierre! Did you hear what he said?

EMIL GRELIEU

Significantly.

Jeanne!

JEANNE

What? No, no—why do you look at me this way? No—I am telling you.

Pierre brings her water, but Jeanne does not drink it.

JEANNE

Thank you, Pierre, but I don't want it.

Silence.

How fragrant the flowers are. Pierre, please give me that rose—yes, that one. Thank you. How fresh it is, Emil, and what a fine fragrance—come over here, Emil!

Emil Grelieu goes over to her and kisses the hand in which she holds the rose. Looks at her.

JEANNE

Lowering her hand.

No; I have asked for this flower simply because its fragrance seems to me immortal—it is always the same—as the sky. How strange it is, always the same. And when you bring it close to your face, and close to your eyes, it seems to you that there is nothing except this red rose and the blue sky. Nothing but the red rose and the distant, pale—very pale—blue sky....

EMIL GRELIEU

Pierre! Listen to me, my boy! People speak of this only at night, when they are alone with their souls—and she knows it, but you do not know it yet. Don't you know it, Jeanne?

JEANNE

Trembling, opening her eyes.

Yes, I know, Emil.

EMIL GRELIEU

21

The life of the poet does not belong to him. The roof over the heads of people, which shelters them—all that is a phantom for me, and my life does not belong to me. I am always far away, not here—I am always where I am not. You think of finding me among the living, while I am dead; you are afraid of finding me in death, mute, cold, doomed to decay, while I live and sing aloud from my grave. Death which makes people mute, which leaves the imprint of silence upon the bravest lips, restores the voice to the poet. Dead, I speak more loudly than alive. Dead, I am alive! Am I—just think of it, Pierre, my boy,—am I to fear death when in my most persistent searches I could not find the boundary between life and death, when in my feelings I mix life and death into one—as two strong, rare kinds of wine? Just think of it, my boy!

Silence. Emil Grelieu looks at his son, smiling. Pierre has covered his face with his hands. The woman is apparently calm. She turns her eyes from her weeping son to her husband.

PIERRE

Uncovering his face.

Forgive me, father!

JEANNE

Take this rose, Pierre, and when it fades and falls apart tear down another rose—it will have the same fragrance as this one. You are a foolish little boy, Pierre, but I am also foolish, although Emil is so kind that he thinks differently. Will you be in the same regiment, Emil?

EMIL GRELIEU

No, hardly, Jeanne.

PIERRE

Father, it is better that we be in the same regiment. I will arrange it, father—will you permit me? And I will teach you how to march—. You know, I am going to be your superior officer.

EMIL GRELIEU

Smiling.

Very well.

JEANNE

Goes out singing in a low voice.

"Only the halo of the arts is crowning—law, liberty, and the King." Who is that? Ah, you! Look, Pierre, here is the girl you wished to see. Come in, come in, my dear child! Don't be afraid, come in! You know him. That's my husband. He is a very good man and will do you no harm. And this is my son, Pierre. Give him your hand.

A girl enters; she is frail, very pale, and beautiful. She wears a black dress, her hair is combed neatly, and she is modest in her demeanor. Her eyes reflect fright and sorrow. She is followed by the chambermaid, Silvina, a kind, elderly woman in a white cap; by Madame Henrietta, and another woman in the service of the Grelieu household. They stop at the threshold and watch the girl curiously. The elder woman is weeping as she looks at her.

GIRL

Stretching forth her hand to Pierre.

Oh, that is a soldier! Be so kind, soldier, tell me how to go to Lonua. I have lost my way.

PIERRE

Confused.

I do not know, Mademoiselle.

GIRL

Looking at everybody mournfully.

Who knows? It is time for me to go.

JEANNE

Cautiously and tenderly leading her to a seat.

Sit down, child, take a rest, my dear, give your poor feet a rest. Pierre, her feet are wounded, yet she wants to walk all the time.

ELDERLY WOMAN

I wanted to stop her, Monsieur Pierre, but it is impossible to stop her. If we close the door before her the poor girl beats her head against the walls, like a bird in a cage. Poor girl!

Dries her tears. François enters from the garden and occupies himself again with the flowers. He glances at the girl from time to time. It is evident that he is making painful efforts to hear and understand what is going on.

GIRL

It is time for me to go.

JEANNE

Rest yourself, here, my child! Why should you leave? At night it is so terrible on the roads. There, in the dark air, bullets are buzzing instead of our dear bees; there wicked people, vicious beasts are roaming. And there is no one who can tell you, for there is no one who knows how to go to Lonua.

GIRL

Don't you know how I could find my way to Lonua?

PIERRE

Softly.

What is she asking?

EMIL GRELIEU

Oh, you may speak louder; she can hear as little as François. She is asking about the village which the Prussians have set on fire. Her home used to be there—now there are only ruins and corpses there. There is no road that leads to Lonua!

GIRL

Don't you know it, either? No one knows. I have asked everybody, and no one can tell me how to find my way to Lonua. I must hurry. They are waiting for me there.

She rises quickly and walks over to François.

Tell me; you are kindhearted! Don't you know the way to Lonua?

François looks at her intently. Silently he turns away and walks out, stooping.

JEANNE

Seating her again.

Sit down, little girl. He does not know.

GIRL

Sadly.

I am asking, and they are silent.

EMIL GRELIEU

I suppose she is also asking the bodies of the dead that lie in the fields and in the ditches how to go to Lonua.

JEANNE

Her hands and her dress were bloodstained. She was walking all night. Take a rest, my little one! I will hold you in my arms, and you will feel better and more comfortable, my little child.

GIRL

Softly.

Tell me, how can I find my way to Lonua?

JEANNE

Yes, yes, come! Emil, I will go with her to my room. There she will feel more comfortable. Come along, my dear. I'll hold you. Come!

They go out. The other women follow them. Emil Grelieu and Pierre remain.

EMIL GRELIEU

Lonua! A quiet little village which no one ever noticed before—houses, trees, and flowers. Where is it now? Who knows the way to that little village? Pierre, the soul of our people is roaming about in the watches of the night, asking the dead how to find the way to Lonua! Pierre, I cannot endure it any longer! I am suffocating from hatred and anger! Oh, weep, you German Nation—bitter will be the fate of your children, terrible will be your disgrace before the judgment of the free nations!

Curtain

SCENE III

Night. The dark silhouette of Emil Grelieu's villa stands out in the background. The gatekeeper's house is seen among the trees, a dim light in the window. At the cast-iron fence frightened women are huddled together, watching the fire in the distance. An alarming redness has covered the sky; only in the zenith is the sky dark. The reflection of the fire falls upon objects and people, casting strange shadows against the mirrors of the mute and dark villa. The voices sound muffled and timid; there are frequent pauses and prolonged sighs. Three women.

HENRIETTA

My God, my God! How terrible it is! It is burning and burning, and there is no end to the fire!

SECOND WOMAN

Yesterday it was burning further away, and tonight the fire is nearer. It is growing nearer. O Lord!

HENRIETTA

It is burning and burning, there is no end to the fire! Today the sun was covered in a mist.

SECOND WOMAN

It is forever burning, and the sun is growing ever darker! Now it is lighter at night than in the daytime!

SILVINA

I am afraid!

HENRIETTA

Be silent, Silvina, be silent!

Silence.

SECOND WOMAN

I can't hear a sound. What is binning there? If I close my eyes it seems to me that nothing is going on there. It is so quiet! Even the dogs are not barking!

HENRIETTA

I can see all that is going on there even with my eyes closed. Look; it seems the fire is spreading!

SILVINA

Oh, I am afraid!

SECOND WOMAN *Where is it burning?*

HENRIETTA

I don't know. It is burning and burning, and there is no end to the fire! It may be that they have all perished by this time. It may be that something terrible is going on there, and we are looking on and know nothing.

A fourth woman approaches them quietly.

FOURTH WOMAN

Good evening!

SILVINA

With restraint.

Oh!

HENRIETTA

Oh, you have frightened us! Good evening, neighbor!

FOURTH WOMAN

Good evening, Madame Henrietta! Never mind my coming here—it is terrible to stay in the house! I guessed that you were not sleeping, but here, watching. You can see well from this spot. Don't you know where the fire is?

SECOND WOMAN

No. And we can't hear a sound—how quiet!

HENRIETTA

It is burning and burning. Haven't you heard anything about your husband?

FOURTH WOMAN

No, nothing. I have already stopped weeping.

HENRIETTA

And with whom are your children just now?

FOURTH WOMAN

Alone. They are asleep. Is it true that Monsieur Pierre was killed? I've heard about it.

HENRIETTA

Agitated.

Just imagine! I don't know! I simply cannot understand what is going on! You see, there is no one in the house now, and we are afraid to sleep there—

SECOND WOMAN

The three of us sleep here, in the gatekeeper's house.

HENRIETTA

I am afraid to look into that house even in the daytime—the house is so large and so empty! And there are no men there, not a soul—

FOURTH WOMAN

Is it true that François has gone to shoot the Prussians? I have heard about it.

HENRIETTA

Maybe. Everybody is talking about it, but we don't know. He disappeared quietly, like a mouse.

FOURTH WOMAN

He will be hanged—the Prussians hang such people!

HENRIETTA

Wait, wait! Today, while I was in the garden, I heard the telephone ringing in the house; it was ringing for a long time. I was frightened, but I went in after all—and, just think of it! Some one said: "Monsieur Pierre was killed!"

SECOND WOMAN

And nothing more?

HENRIETTA

Nothing more; not a word! All grew quiet again. I felt so bad and was so frightened that I could hardly run out. Now I will not enter that house for anything!

FOURTH WOMAN

Whose voice was it?

SECOND WOMAN

Madame Henrietta says it was an unfamiliar voice.

HENRIETTA

Yes, an unfamiliar voice.

FOURTH WOMAN

Look! There seems to be a light in the windows of the house—somebody is there!

SILVINA

Oh, I am afraid! I can't bear it!

HENRIETTA

Oh, what are you saying; what are you saying? There is no one there!

SECOND WOMAN

That's from the redness of the sky!

FOURTH WOMAN

What if some one is ringing there again?

HENRIETTA

How is that possible? At night?

All listen. Silence.

SECOND WOMAN

What will become of us? They are coming this way, and there is nothing that can stop them!

FOURTH WOMAN

I wish I might die now! When you are dead, you don't hear or see anything.

HENRIETTA

It keeps on all night like this—it is burning and burning! And in the daytime it will again be hard to see things on account of the smoke; and the bread will smell of burning! What is going on there?

FOURTH WOMAN

They have killed Monsieur Pierre.

SECOND WOMAN

They have killed him? Killed him?

SILVINA

You must not speak of it! My God, whither should I go! I cannot bear this. I cannot understand it!

Weeps softly.

FOURTH WOMAN

They say there are twenty millions of them, and they have already set Paris on fire. They say they have cannon which can hit a hundred kilometers away.

HENRIETTA

My God, my God! And all that is coming upon us!

SECOND WOMAN

Merciful God, have pity on us!

FOURTH WOMAN

And they are flying and they are hurling bombs from airships—terrible bombs, which destroy entire cities!

HENRIETTA

My God! What have they done with the sky! Before this You were alone in the sky, and now those base Prussians are there too!

SECOND WOMAN

Before this, when my soul wanted rest and joy I looked at the sky, but now there is no place where a poor soul can find rest and joy!

FOURTH WOMAN

They have taken everything away from our Belgium—even the sky! I wish I could die at once! There is no air to breathe now!

Suddenly frightened.

Listen! Don't you think that now my husband, my husband—

HENRIETTA

No, no!

FOURTH WOMAN

Why is the sky so red? What is it that is burning there?

SECOND WOMAN

Have mercy on us, O God! The fire seems to be moving toward us!

Silence. The redness of the flames seems to be swaying over the earth.

Curtain

SCENE IV

Dawn. The sun has already risen, but it is hidden behind the heavy mist and smoke. A large room in Emil Grelieu's villa, which has been turned into a sickroom. There are two wounded there, Grelieu himself, with a serious wound in his shoulder, and his son Maurice, with a light wound on his right arm. The large window, covered with half transparent curtains, admits a faint bluish light. The wounded appear to be asleep. In an armchair at the bedside of Grelieu there is a motionless figure in white, Jeanne.

EMIL GRELIEU

Softly.

Jeanne!

She leans over the bed quickly.

JEANNE

Shall I give you some water?

EMIL GRELIEU

No. You are tired.

JEANNE

Oh, no, not at all. I was dozing all night. Can't you fall asleep, Emil?

EMIL GRELIEU

What time is it?

She goes over to the window quietly, and pushing the curtain aside slightly, looks at her little watch. Then she returns just as quietly.

JEANNE

It is still early. Perhaps you will try to fall asleep, Emil? It seems to me that you have been suffering great pain; you have been groaning all night.

EMIL GRELIEU

No, I am feeling better. How is the weather this morning?

JEANNE

Nasty weather, Emil; you can't see the sun. Try to sleep.

Silence. Suddenly Maurice utters a cry in his sleep; the cry turns into a groan and indistinct mumbling. Jeanne walks over to him and listens, then returns to her seat.

EMIL GRELIEU

Is the boy getting on well?

JEANNE

Don't worry, Emil. He only said a few words in his sleep.

EMIL GRELIEU

He has done it several times tonight.

JEANNE

I am afraid that he is disturbing you. We can have him removed to another room and Henrietta will stay with him. The boy's blood is in good condition. In another week, I believe, we shall be able to remove the bandage from his arm.

29

EMIL GRELIEU

No, let him stay here, Jeanne.

JEANNE

What is it, my dear?

She kneels at his bed and kisses his hand carefully.

EMIL GRELIEU

Jeanne!

JEANNE

I think your fever has gone down, my dear.

Impresses another kiss upon his hand and clings to it.

EMIL GRELIEU

You are my love, Jeanne.

JEANNE

Do not speak, do not speak. Don't agitate yourself.

A brief moment of silence.

EMIL GRELIEU

Moving his head restlessly.

It is so hard to breathe here, the air——

JEANNE

The window has been open all night, my dear. There is not a breeze outside.

EMIL GRELIEU

There is smoke.

JEANNE

Yes.

MAURICE

Utters a cry once more, then mutters—

Stop, stop, stop!

Again indistinctly.

It is burning, it is burning! Oh! Who is going to the battery, who is going to the battery——

He mutters and then grows silent.

EMIL GRELIEU

What painful dreams!

JEANNE

That's nothing; the boy always used to talk in his sleep. Yesterday he looked so well.

EMIL GRELIEU

Jeanne!

JEANNE

What is it, my dear?

EMIL GRELIEU

Sit down.

JEANNE

Very well.

EMIL GRELIEU

Jeanne.... Are you thinking about Pierre?

Silence.

JEANNE

Softly.

Don't speak of him.

EMIL GRELIEU

You are right. Death is not so terrible. Isn't that true, Jeanne?

JEANNE

After a brief pause.

That's true.

EMIL GRELIEU

We shall follow him later. He will not come here, but we shall go to him. I was thinking of it at night. It is so clear. Do you remember the red rose which you gave him? I remember it.

JEANNE

Yes.

EMIL GRELIEU

It is so clear. Jeanne, lean over me. You are the best woman in the world.

Silence.

EMIL GRELIEU

Tossing about in his bed.

It is so hard to breathe.

JEANNE

My dear——
EMIL GRELIEU

No, that's nothing. The night is tormenting me. Jeanne, was I dreaming, or have I really heard cannonading?
JEANNE

You really heard it, at about five o'clock. But very far away, Emil—it was hardly audible. Close your eyes, my dear, rest yourself.
Silence
MAURICE

Faintly.
Mamma!
Jeanne walks over to him quietly.
JEANNE

Are you awake?
MAURICE

Yes. I have slept enough. How is father?
JEANNE

He is awake.
EMIL GRELIEU

Good morning, Maurice.
MAURICE

Good morning, papa. How do you feel? I am feeling well.
EMIL GRELIEU

I, too, am feeling well. Jeanne, you may draw the curtain aside. I can't sleep any longer.
JEANNE

Very well. What a nasty day! Still it will be easier for you to breathe when it is light.
She draws the curtain aside slowly, so as not to make it too light at once. Beyond the large window vague silhouettes of the trees are seen at the window frames and several withered, bent flowers. Maurice is trying to adjust the screen.
JEANNE

What are you doing, Maurice?
MAURICE

My coat—Never mind, I'll fix it myself.
Guiltily.
No, mamma, you had better help me.
JEANNE

Going behind the screen.
What a foolish boy you are, Maurice.
Behind the screen.
Be careful, be careful, that's the way. Don't hurry, be careful.
MAURICE

Behind the screen.

Pin this for me right here, as you did yesterday. That's very good.

JEANNE

Behind the screen.

Of course. Wait, you'll kiss me later—. Well? That's the way.

Maurice comes out, his right arm dressed in a bandage. He goes over to his father and first kisses his hand, then, upon a sign from his eyes, he kisses him on the lips.

EMIL GRELIEU

Good morning, good morning, my dear boy.

MAURICE

Looking around at the screen, where his mother is putting the bed in order.

Papa, look!

He takes his hand out of the bandage and straightens it quickly. Then he puts it back just as quickly. Emil Grelieu threatens him with his finger. Jeanne puts the screen aside, and the bed is already in order.

JEANNE

I am through now. Maurice, come to the bathroom. I'll wash you.

MAURICE

Oh, no; under no circumstances. I'll wash myself today. Last night I washed myself with my left hand and it was very fine.

Walking over to the open window.

How nasty it is. These scoundrels have spoiled the day. Still, it is warm and there is the smell of flowers. It's good, papa; it is very fine.

EMIL GRELIEU

Yes, it is pleasant.

MAURICE

Well, I am going.

JEANNE

Clean your teeth; you didn't do it yesterday, Maurice.

MAURICE

Grumbling.

What's the use of it now? Very well, I'll do it.

At the door.

Papa, do you know, well have good news today; I feel it.

He is heard calling in a ringing voice, "Silvina."

EMIL GRELIEU

I feel better.

JEANNE

I'll let you have your coffee directly. You are looking much better today, much better.

EMIL GRELIEU

What is this?

JEANNE

Perfume, with water. I'll bathe your face with it That's the way. Now I again have little children to wash. You see how pleasant it feels.

EMIL GRELIEU

Yes. What did he say about good news?

JEANNE

He didn't mean anything. He is very happy because he is a hero.

EMIL GRELIEU

Do you know any news?

JEANNE

Irresolutely.

Nothing. What news could there be?

EMIL GRELIEU

Tell me, Jeanne; you were firmer before. Tell me my dear.

JEANNE

Was I firmer? Perhaps.... I have grown accustomed to talk to you softly at night. Well—how shall I tell it to you? They are coming.

EMIL GRELIEU

Coming?

JEANNE

Yes. You know their numbers and ours. Don't be excited, but I think that it will be necessary for us to leave for Antwerp today.

EMIL GRELIEU

Are they near?

JEANNE

Yes, they are near. Very near.

Sings softly.

"Le Roi, la Loi, la Liberté." Very near. I have not told you that the King inquired yesterday about your health. I answered that you were feeling better and that you will be able to leave today.

EMIL GRELIEU

Of course I am able to leave today. And what did he say about them?

JEANNE

What did the King say?

Singing the same tune.

He said that their numbers were too great.

EMIL GRELIEU

What else did he say? What else, Jeanne?

JEANNE

What else? He said that there was a God and there was righteousness. That's what I believe I heard him say—that there was still a God and that righteousness was still in existence. How old these words are, Emil! But it is so good that they still exist.

Silence.

EMIL GRELIEU

Yes, in the daytime you are so different. Where do you get so much strength, Jeanne?

JEANNE

Where?

EMIL GRELIEU

I am forever looking at your hair. I am wondering why it hasn't turned gray.

JEANNE

I dye it at night, Emil. I'll bring in some more flowers. Now it is very cozy here. Oh, yes, I haven't told you yet—some one will be here to see you today—Secretary Lagard and some one else by the name of Count Clairmont.

EMIL GRELIEU

Count Clairmont? I don't know him.

JEANNE

It is not necessary that you should know him. He is simply known as Count Clairmont, Count Clairmont—. That's a good name for a very good man.

EMIL GRELIEU

I know a very good man in Belgium—

JEANNE

Tsh! You must not know anything. You must only remember—Count Clairmont. They have some important matters to discuss with you, I believe. And they'll send you an automobile, to take you to Antwerp.

EMIL GRELIEU

Smiling.

Count Clairmont?

JEANNE

Also smiling.

Yes. You are loved by everybody, but if I were a King, I would have sent you an aeroplane.

Throwing back her hands in sorrow which she is trying vainly to suppress.

Ah, how good it would be now to rise from the ground and fly—and fly for a long, long time.

Enter Maurice.

MAURICE

I am ready now, I have cleaned my teeth. I've even taken a walk in the garden. But I have never before noticed that we have such a beautiful garden! Papa, our garden is wonderfully beautiful!

JEANNE

Coffee will be ready directly. If he disturbs you with his talk, call me, Emil.

MAURICE

Oh, I did not mean to disturb you. Forgive me, papa. I'll not disturb you any more.

EMIL GRELIEU

35

You may speak, speak. I am feeling quite well, quite well.

JEANNE

But you must save your strength, don't forget that, Emil.

Exit.

MAURICE

Sitting down quietly at the window.

Perhaps I really ought not to speak, papa?

EMIL GRELIEU

Smiling faintly.

Can you be silent?

MAURICE

Blushing.

No, father, I cannot just now. I suppose I seem to you very young.

EMIL GRELIEU

And what do you think of it yourself?

MAURICE

Blushing again.

I am no longer as young as I was three weeks ago. Yes, only three weeks ago—I remember the tolling of the bells in our church, I remember how I teased François. How strange that François has been lost and no one knows where he is. What does it mean that a human being is lost and no one knows where he is? Before, one could see everything on earth.

EMIL GRELIEU

Yes.

MAURICE

Papa! Why do they hang such people as François? That is cruel and stupid. Forgive me for speaking so harshly. But need an old man love his fatherland less than I love it, for instance? The old people love it even more intensely. Let everyone fight as he can. I am not tiring you, am I? An old man came to us, he was very feeble, he asked for bullets—well, let them hang me too—I gave him bullets. A few of our regiment made sport of him, but he said: "If only one Prussian bullet will strike me, it means that the Prussians will have one bullet less." That appealed to me.

EMIL GRELIEU

Yes, that appeals to me, too. Have you heard the cannonading at dawn?

MAURICE

No. Why, was there any cannonading?

EMIL GRELIEU

Yes. I heard cannonading. Did mamma tell you that they are coming nearer and nearer? They are approaching.

MAURICE

Rising.

36

Really? Impossible!
EMIL GRELIEU

They are coming, and we must leave for Antwerp today.
MAURICE

Yes.

He rises and walks back and forth, forgetting his wounded arm. He is greatly agitated. Clenches his fist.
MAURICE

Father, tell me: What do you think of the present state of affairs?
EMIL GRELIEU

Mamma says there is a God and there is righteousness.
MAURICE

Raising his hand.

Mamma says——Let God bless mamma! I don't know—I—. Very well, very well. We shall see; we shall see!

His face twitches like a child's face. He is trying to repress his tears.
MAURICE

I still owe them something for Pierre. Forgive me, father; I don't know whether I have a right to say this or not, but I am altogether different from you. It is wicked but I can't help it. I was looking this morning at your flowers in the garden and I felt so sorry—sorry for you, because you had grown them. Those rascals!
EMIL GRELIEU

Maurice!
MAURICE

The scoundrels! I don't want to consider them human beings, and I shall not consider them human beings.

Enter Jeanne.
JEANNE

What is it, Maurice? That isn't right.
MAURICE

Very well.

As he passes he embraces his mother with his left hand and kisses her.
JEANNE

You had better sit down. It is dangerous for your health to walk around this way.
EMIL GRELIEU

Sit down, Maurice.

Maurice sits down at the window facing the garden. Emil Grelieu smiles sadly and closes his eyes. Silvina, the maid, brings in coffee and sets it on the table near Grelieu's bed.
SILVINA

Good morning, Monsieur Emil.
EMIL GRELIEU

Opening his eyes.

Good morning, Silvina.

Exit Silvina.

JEANNE

Go and have your breakfast, Maurice.

MAURICE

Without turning around.

I don't want any breakfast. Mamma, I'll take off my bandage tomorrow.

JEANNE

Laughing.

Soldier, is it possible that you are capricious?

Silence. Jeanne helps Emil Grelieu with his coffee.

JEANNE

That's the way. Is it convenient for you this way, or do you want to drink it with a spoon?

EMIL GRELIEU

Oh, my poor head, it is so weak—

MAURICE

Going over to him.

Forgive me, father, I'll not do it any more. I was foolishly excited, but do you know I could not endure it. May I have a cup, mamma?

JEANNE

Yes, this is yours. You feel better now?

MAURICE

Yes, I do.

EMIL GRELIEU

I am feeling perfectly well today, Jeanne. When is the bandage to be changed?

JEANNE

Later. Count Clairmont will bring his surgeon along with him.

MAURICE

Who is that, mamma? Have I seen him?

JEANNE

You'll see him. But, please, Maurice, when you see him, don't open your mouth so wide. You have a habit—you open your mouth and then you forget about it.

MAURICE

Blushing.

You are both looking at me and smiling. But I have time yet to grow. I have time yet to grow.

The sound of automobiles is heard.

JEANNE

Rising quickly.

38

I think they are here. Maurice, this is only Count Clairmont, don't forget. I'll be back directly. They will speak with you about a very, very important matter, Emil, but you must not be agitated.

EMIL GRELIEU

Yes, I know.

JEANNE

Kissing him quickly.

I am going.

Exit, almost colliding with Silvina, who is excited.

MAURICE

Whispering.

Who is it, Silvina?

Silvina makes some answer in mingled delight and awe. Maurice's face assumes the same expression as Silvina's. Silvina goes out. Maurice walks quickly to the window and raises his left hand to his forehead, straightening himself in military fashion. Thus he stands until the others notice him.

Enter Jeanne, Count Clairmont, followed by Secretary Lagard and the Count's adjutant, an elderly General of stem appearance, with numerous decorations upon his chest. The Count himself is tall, well built and young, in a modest officer's uniform, without any medals to signify his high station. He carries himself very modestly, almost bashfully, but overcoming his first uneasiness, he speaks warmly and powerfully and freely. His gestures are swift. All treat him with profound respect. Lagard is a strong old man with a leonine gray head. He speaks simply, his gestures are calm and resolute. It is evident that he is in the habit of speaking from a platform. Jeanne holds a large bouquet of flowers in her hands. Count Clairmont walks directly toward Grelieu's bedside.

COUNT CLAIRMONT

Confused.

I have come to shake hands with you, my dear master. Oh, but do not make a single unnecessary movement, not a single one, otherwise I shall be very unhappy!

EMIL GRELIEU

I am deeply moved, I am happy.

COUNT CLAIRMONT

No, no, don't speak that way. Here stands before you only a man who has learned to think from your books. But see what they have done to you—look, Lagard!

LAGARD

How are you, Grelieu? I, too, want to shake your hand. Today I am a Secretary by the will of Fate, but yesterday I was only a physician, and I may congratulate you—you have a kind hand. Let me feel your pulse.

GENERAL

Coming forward modestly.

Allow me, too, in the name of this entire army of ours to express to you our admiration, Monsieur Grelieu!

EMIL GRELIEU

I thank you. I am feeling perfectly well, Lagard.

COUNT CLAIRMONT

But perhaps it is necessary to have a surgeon?

JEANNE

He can listen and talk, Count. He is smiling—he can listen.

COUNT CLAIRMONT

Noticing Maurice, confused.

Oh! who is this? Please put down your hand—you are wounded.

MAURICE

I am so happy, Count.

JEANNE

This is our second son. Our first son, Pierre, was killed at Liège—

COUNT CLAIRMONT

I dare not console you, Madame Grelieu. Give me your hand, Maurice.

MAURICE

Oh, Count! I am only a soldier. I dare not—

COUNT CLAIRMONT

My dear young man, I, too, am nothing but a soldier now. Your hand, comrade. That's the way. Master! My children and my wife have sent you flowers—but where are they? Oh! how absentminded I am.

JEANNE

Here they are, Count.

COUNT CLAIRMONT

Thank you. But I did not know that your flowers were better than mine, for my flowers smell of smoke.

LAGARD

Like all Belgium.

To Count Clairmont.

His pulse is good. Grelieu, we have come to you not only to express our sympathy. Through me all the working people of Belgium are shaking your hand.

EMIL GRELIEU

I am proud of it, Lagard.

LAGARD

But we are just as proud. Yes; there is something we must discuss with you. Count Clairmont did not wish to disturb you, but I said: "Let him die, but before that we must speak to him." Isn't that so, comrade?

EMIL GRELIEU

I am not dying. Maurice, I think you had better go out.

40

COUNT CLAIRMONT

Quickly.

Oh, no, no. He is your son, Grelieu, and he should be present to hear what his father will say. Oh, I should have been proud to have such a father.

LAGARD

Our Count is a very fine young man—Pardon me, Count, I have again upset our—

COUNT CLAIRMONT

That's nothing, I have already grown accustomed to it. Master, it is necessary for you and your family to leave for Antwerp today.

EMIL GRELIEU

Are our affairs in such a critical condition?

LAGARD

What is there to tell? Things are in bad shape, very bad. That horde of Huns is coming upon us like the tide of the sea. Today they are still there, but tomorrow they will flood your house, Grelieu. They are coming toward Antwerp. To what can we resort in our defence? On this side are they, and there is the sea. Only very little is left of Belgium, Grelieu. Very soon there will be no room even for my beard here. Isn't that so, Count?

Silence. Dull sounds of cannonading are heard in the distance. All turn their eyes to the window.

EMIL GRELIEU

Is that a battle?

COUNT CLAIRMONT

Listening, calmly.

No, that is only the beginning. But tomorrow they will carry their devilish weapons past your house. Do you know they are real iron monsters, under whose weight our earth is quaking and groaning. They are moving slowly, like amphibia that have crawled out at night from the abyss—but they are moving! Another few days will pass, and they will crawl over to Antwerp, they will turn their jaws to the city, to the churches—Woe to Belgium, master! Woe to Belgium!

LAGARD

Yes, it is very bad. We are an honest and peaceful people despising bloodshed, for war is such a stupid affair! And we should not have had a single soldier long ago were it not for this accursed neighbor, this den of murderers.

GENERAL

And what would we have done without any soldiers, Monsieur Lagard?

LAGARD

And what can we do with soldiers, Monsieur General?

COUNT CLAIRMONT

You are wrong, Lagard. With our little army there is still one possibility—to die as freemen die. But without an army we would have been bootblacks, Lagard!

41

LAGARD

Grumbling.

Well, I would not clean anybody's boots. Things are in bad shape, Grelieu, in very bad shape. And there is but one remedy left for us—. True, it is a terrible remedy.

EMIL GRELIEU

I know.

LAGARD

Yes? What is it?

EMIL GRELIEU

The dam.

Jeanne and Emil shudder and look at each other with terror in their eyes.

COUNT CLAIRMONT

You shuddered, you are shuddering, madame. But what am I to do, what are we to do, we who dare not shudder?

JEANNE

Oh, I simply thought of a girl who was trying to find her way to Lonua. She will never find her way to Lonua.

COUNT CLAIRMONT

But what is to be done? What is to be done?

All become thoughtful. The Count steps away to the window and looks out, nervously twitching his mustaches. Maurice has moved aside and, as before, stands at attention. Jeanne stands a little distance away from him, with her shoulder leaning against the wall, her beautiful pale head thrown back. Lagard is sitting at the bedside as before, stroking his gray, disheveled beard. The General is absorbed in gloomy thoughts.

COUNT CLAIRMONT

Turning around resolutely.

I am a peaceful man, but I can understand why people take up arms. Arms! That means a sword, a gun, explosive contrivances. That is fire. Fire is killing people, but at the same time it also gives light. Fire cleanses. There is something of the ancient sacrifice in it. But water! cold, dark, silent, covering with mire, causing bodies to swell—water, which was the beginning of chaos; water, which is guarding the earth by day and night in order to rush upon it. My friend, believe me, I am quite a daring man, but I am afraid of water! Lagard, what would you say to that?

LAGARD

We Belgians have too long been struggling against the water not to have learned to fear it. I am also afraid of water.

JEANNE

But what is more terrible, the Prussians or water?

GENERAL

Bowing.

Madame is right. The Prussians are not more terrible, but they are worse.

LAGARD

Yes. We have no other choice. It is terrible to release water from captivity, the beast from its den, nevertheless it is a better friend to us than the Prussians. I would prefer to see the whole of Belgium covered with water rather than extend a hand of reconciliation to a scoundrel! Neither they nor we shall live to see that, even if the entire Atlantic Ocean rush over our heads.

Brief pause.

GENERAL

But I hope that we shall not come to that. Meanwhile it is necessary for us to flood only part of our territory. That is not so terrible.

JEANNE

Her eyes closed, her head hanging down.

And what is to be done with those who could not abandon their homes, who are deaf, who are sick and alone? What will become of our children?

Silence.

JEANNE

There in the fields and in the ditches are the wounded. There the shadows of people are wandering about, but in their veins there is still warm blood. What will become of them? Oh, don't look at me like that, Emil; you had better not listen to what I am saying. I have spoken so only because my heart is wrung with pain—it isn't necessary to listen to me at all, Count.

Count Clairmont walks over to Grelieu's bed quickly and firmly. At first he speaks confusedly, seeking the right word; then he speaks ever more boldly and firmly.

COUNT CLAIRMONT

My dear and honored master! We would not have dared to take from you even a drop of your health, if—if it were not for the assurance that serving your people may give new strength to your heroic soul! Yesterday, it was resolved at our council to break the dams and flood part of our kingdom, but I could not, I dared not, give my full consent before I knew what you had to say to this plan. I did not sleep all night long, thinking—oh, how terrible, how inexpressibly sad my thoughts were! We are the body, we are the hands, we are the head—while you, Grelieu, you are the conscience of our people. Blinded by the war, we may unwillingly, unwittingly, altogether against our will, violate man-made laws. Let your noble heart tell us the truth. My friend! We are driven to despair, we have no Belgium any longer, it is trampled by our enemies, but in your breast, Emil Grelieu, the heart of all Belgium is beating—and your answer will be the answer of our tormented, blood-stained, unfortunate land!

He turns away to the window. Maurice is crying, looking at his father.

LAGARD

Softly.

Bravo, Belgium!

Silence. The sound of cannonading is heard.

JEANNE

Softly, to Maurice.

Sit down, Maurice, it is hard for you to stand.

MAURICE

Oh, mamma! I am so happy to stand here now—

LAGARD

Now I shall add a few words. As you know, Grelieu, I am a man of the people. I know the price the people pay for their hard work. I know the cost of all these gardens, orchards and factories which we shall bury under the water. They have cost us sweat and health and tears, Grelieu. These are our sufferings which will be transformed into joy for our children. But as a nation that loves and respects liberty above its sweat and blood and tears—as a nation, I say, I would prefer that sea waves should seethe here over our heads rather than that we should have to black the boots of the Prussians. And if nothing but islands remain of Belgium they will be known as "honest islands," and the islanders will be Belgians as before.

All are agitated.

EMIL GRELIEU

And what do the engineers say?

GENERAL

Respectfully waiting for the Count's answer.

Monsieur Grelieu, they say this can be done in two hours.

LAGARD

Grumbles.

In two hours! In two hours! How many years have we been building it!

GENERAL

The engineers were crying when they said it, Monsieur.

LAGARD

The engineers were crying? But how could they help crying? Think of it, Grelieu!

Suddenly he bursts into sobs, and slowly takes a handkerchief from his pocket.

COUNT CLAIRMONT

We are awaiting your answer impatiently, Grelieu. You are charged with a grave responsibility to your fatherland—to lift your hand against your own fatherland.

EMIL GRELIEU Have we no other defence?

Silence. All stand in poses of painful anxiety. Lagard dries his eyes and slowly answers with a sigh.

LAGARD

No.

GENERAL

No.
JEANNE
Shaking her head.
No.
COUNT CLAIRMONT
Rapidly.
We must gain time, Grelieu. By the power of all our lives, thrown in the fields, we cannot stop them.
Stamping his foot.
Time, time! We must steal from fate a small part of eternity—a few days, a week! They are hastening to us. The Russians are coming to us from the East. The German steel has already penetrated to the heart of the French land—and infuriated with pain, the French eagle is rising over the Germans' bayonets and is coming toward us! The noble knights of the sea—the British—are already rushing toward us, and to Belgium are their powerful arms stretched out over the abyss. But, time, time! Give us time, Grelieu. Belgium is praying for a few days, for a few hours! You have already given to Belgium your blood, Grelieu, and you have the right to lift your hand against your blood-stained fatherland!
Brief pause.
EMIL GRELIEU
We must break the dams.
Curtain

SCENE V

Night. A small house occupied by the German staff. A sentinel on guard at the door leading to the rooms occupied by the Commander of the army. All the doors and windows are open. The room is illuminated with candles. Two officers on duty are talking lazily, suffering apparently from the heat. All is quiet in the camp. Only from time to time the measured footsteps of pickets are heard, and muffled voices and angry exclamations.

VON RITZAU

Do you feel sleepy, von Stein?

VON STEIN

I don't feel sleepy, but I feel like smoking.

RITZAU

A bad habit! But you may smoke near the window.

STEIN

But what if he should come in? Thank you, von Ritzau. What a stifling night! Not a breath of pure air enters the lungs. The air is poisoned with the smell of smoke. We must invent something against this obnoxious odor. Take it up, Ritzau.

RITZAU

I am not an inventor. First of all it is necessary to wring out the air as they wring the clothes they wash, and dry it in the sun. It is so moist, I feel as though I were diving in it. Do you know whether he is in a good mood today?

STEIN

Why, is he subject to moods, good or bad?

RITZAU

Great self-restraint!

STEIN

Have you ever seen him undressed—or half-dressed? Or have you ever seen his hair in disorder? He is a wonderful old man!

RITZAU

He speaks so devilishly little, Stein.

STEIN

He prefers to have his cannon speak. It is quite a powerful voice, isn't it, Ritzau?

They laugh softly. A tall, handsome officer enters quickly and goes toward the door leading to the room of the Commander.

Blumenfeld! Any news?

The tall officer waves his hand and opens the door cautiously, ready to make his bow.

He is malting his career!

RITZAU

He is a good fellow. I can't bear it, Stein. I am suffocating here.

STEIN

Would you rather be in Paris?

RITZAU

I would prefer any less unbearable country to this. How dull it must be here in the winter time.

STEIN

But we have saved them from dullness for a long time to come. Were you ever in the Montmartre cafés, Ritzau?

RITZAU

Of course!

STEIN

Doesn't one find there a wonderful refinement, culture and innate elegance? Unfortunately, our Berlin people are far different.

RITZAU

Oh, of course. Great!

The tall officer comes out of the door, stepping backward. He heaves a sigh of relief and sits down near the two officers. Takes out a cigar.

VON BLUMENFELD

How are things?

RITZAU

Very well. We were talking of Paris.

STEIN

Then I am going to smoke too.

BLUMENFELD

You may smoke. He is not coming out Do you want to hear important news?

STEIN

Well?

BLUMENFELD He laughed just now I

STEIN

Really!

BLUMENFELD

Upon my word of honor! And he touched my shoulder with two fingers—do you understand?

STEIN

With envy.

Of course! I suppose you brought him good news, Blumenfeld?

The military telegraphist, standing at attention, hands Blumenfeld a folded paper.

TELEGRAPHIST A radiogram, Lieutenant!

BLUMENFELD

Let me have it.

Slowly he puts his cigar on the window sill and enters the Commander's room cautiously.

STEIN

He's a lucky fellow. You may say what you please about luck, but it exists. Who is this Blumenfeld? Von?—Did you know his father? Or his grandfather?

RITZAU

I have reason to believe that he had no grandfather at all. But he is a good comrade. Blumenfeld comes out and rejoins the two officers, taking up his cigar.

STEIN

Another military secret?

BLUMENFELD

Of course. Everything that is said and done here is a military secret. But I may tell you about it. The information we have received concerns our new siege guns—they are advancing successfully.

STEIN

Oho!

BLUMENFELD

Yes, successfully. They have just passed the most difficult part of the road—you know where the swamps are—

STEIN

Oh, yes.

RITZAU

Great!

BLUMENFELD

The road could not support the heavy weight and caved in. Our commander was very uneasy. He ordered a report about the movement at each and every kilometer.

STEIN

Now he will sleep in peace.

BLUMENFELD

He never sleeps, von Stein.

STEIN

That's true.

BLUMENFELD

He never sleeps, von Stein! When he is not listening to reports or issuing commands, he is thinking. As the personal correspondent of his Highness I have the honor to know many things which others are not allowed to know—Oh, gentlemen, he has a wonderful mind!

RITZAU

Great!

Another very young officer enters, stands at attention before Blumenfeld.

BLUMENFELD

Sit down, von Schauss. I am talking about our Commander.

SCHAUSS

Oh!

BLUMENFELD

He has a German philosophical mind which manages guns as Leibnitz managed ideas. Everything is preconceived, everything is prearranged, the movement of our millions of people has been elaborated into such a remarkable system that Kant himself would have been proud of it. Gentlemen, we are led forward by indomitable logic and by an iron will. We are inexorable as Fate.

The officers express their approval by subdued exclamations of "bravo."

BLUMENFELD

How can he sleep, if the movement of our armies is but the movement of parts of his brains! And what is the use of sleep in general? I sleep very little myself, and I advise you, gentlemen, not to indulge in foolish sleep.

RITZAU

But our human organism requires sleep.

BLUMENFELD

Nonsense! Organism—that is something invented by the doctors who are looking for practice among the fools. I know of no organism. I know only my desires and my will, which says: "Gerhardt, do this! Gerhardt, go there! Gerhardt, take this!" And I take it!

RITZAU

Great!

SCHAUSS

Will you permit me to take down your words in my notebook?

BLUMENFELD

Please, Schauss. What is it you want, Zigler?

The telegraphist has entered.

ZIGLER

I really don't know, but something strange has happened. It seems that we are being interfered with, I can't understand anything.

BLUMENFELD

What is it? What is the matter?

ZIGLER

We can make out one word, "Water"—but after that all is incomprehensible. And then again, "Water"—

BLUMENFELD

What water? You are intoxicated, Zigler. That must be wine, not water. Is the engineer there?

ZIGLER

He is also surprised and cannot understand.

BLUMENFELD

You are a donkey, Zigler! We'll have to call out—

The Commander comes out. He is a tall, erect old man. His face is pale. His voice is dry and unimpassioned.

COMMANDER

Blumenfeld!

49

All jump up, straighten themselves, as if petrified.

What is this?

BLUMENFELD

I have not yet investigated it, your Highness. Zigler is reporting—

COMMANDER

What is it, Zigler?

ZIGLER

Your Highness, we are being interfered with. I don't know what it is, but I can't understand anything. We have been able to make out only one word—"Water." Then again—"Water."

COMMANDER

Turning around.

See what it is, Blumenfeld, and report to me—

Engineer runs in.

ENGINEER

Where is Blumenfeld? I beg your pardon, your Highness!

COMMANDER

Pausing.

What has happened there, Kloetz?

ENGINEER

They don't respond to our calls, your Highness. They are silent like the dead. Something has happened there.

COMMANDER

You think something serious has happened?

ENGINEER

I dare not think so, your Highness, but I am alarmed. Silence is the only answer to our most energetic calls. But Greitzer wishes to say something. ... Well? What is it, Greitzer?

The second telegraphist has entered quietly.

GREITZER

They are silent, your Highness.

Brief pause.

COMMANDER

Again turning to the door.

Please investigate this, Lieutenant.

He advances a step to the door, then stops. There is a commotion behind the windows—a noise and the sound of voices. The word "water" is repeated frequently. The noise keeps growing, turning at times into a loud roar.

What is that?

All turn to the window. An officer, bareheaded, rushes in excitedly, his hair disheveled, his face pale.

OFFICER

I want to see his Highness. I want to see his Highness!

BLUMENFELD

Hissing.

You are insane!

COMMANDER

Calm yourself, officer.

OFFICER

Your Highness! I have the honor to report to you that the Belgians have burst the dams, and our armies are flooded. Water!

With horror.

We must hurry, your Highness!

COMMANDER

Hurry! I ask you to calm yourself, officer. What about our guns?

OFFICER

They are flooded, your Highness.

COMMANDER

Compose yourself, you are not behaving properly! I am asking you about our field guns—

OFFICER

They are flooded, your Highness. The water is coming this way. We must hurry, your Highness, we are in a valley. This place is very low. They have broken the dams; and the water is rushing this way violently. It is only five kilometers away from here—and we can hardly—. I beg your pardon, your Highness!

Silence. The commotion without is growing louder. Glimmering lights appear. The beginning of a terrible panic is felt, embracing the entire camp. All watch impatiently the reddening face of the Commander.

COMMANDER

But this is—

He strikes the table with his fist forcibly.

Absurd!

He looks at them with cold fury, but all lower their eyes. The frightened officer is trembling and gazing at the window. The lights grow brighter outside—it is evident that a building has been set on fire. The voices without have turned into a roar. A dull noise, then the crash of shots is heard. The discipline is disappearing gradually.

BLUMENFELD

They have gone mad!

OFFICER

They are firing! It is an attack!

STEIN

But that can't be the Belgians!

RITZAU

They may have availed themselves—
BLUMENFELD
Aren't you ashamed, Stein? Aren't you ashamed, gentlemen?
COMMANDER *Silence! I beg of you—*
Suddenly a piercing, wild sound of a horn is heard ordering to retreat. The roaring sound is growing rapidly.
COMMANDER
Shots.
Who has commanded to retreat? Who dares command when I am here? What a disgrace, Blumenfeld! Order them to return!
Blumenfeld lowers his head.
COMMANDER
This is not the German Army! You are unworthy of being called soldiers! Shame! I am ashamed to call myself your general! Cowards!
BLUMENFELD
Stepping forward, with dignity.
Your Highness!
OFFICER
Eh! We are not fishes to swim in the water!
Runs out, followed by two or three others. The panic is growing.
BLUMENFELD
Your Highness! We ask you—. Your life is in danger—your Highness.
Some one else runs out. The room is almost empty. Only the sentinel remains in the position of one petrified.
BLUMENFELD
Your Highness! I implore you. Your life—I am afraid that another minute, and it will be too late! Oh, your Highness!
COMMANDER
But this is—
Again strikes the table with his fist.
But this is absurd, Blumenfeld!
Curtain

SCENE VI

The same hour of night. In the darkness it is difficult to discern the silhouettes of the ruined buildings and of the trees. At the right, a half-destroyed bridge. In the distance a fire is burning. From time to time the German flashlights are seen across the dark sky. Near the bridge, an automobile in which the wounded Emil Grelieu and his son are being carried to Antwerp. Jeanne and a young physician are with them. Something has broken down in the automobile and a soldier-chauffeur is bustling about with a lantern trying to repair it. Dr. Langloi stands near him.

DOCTOR

Uneasily.

Well? How is it?

CHAUFFEUR

Examining.

I don't know yet.

DOCTOR

Is it a serious break?

CHAUFFEUR

No—I don't know.

MAURICE

From the automobile.

What is it, Doctor? Can't we start?

CHAUFFEUR

Angrily.

We'll start!

DOCTOR

I don't know. Something is out of order. He says it isn't serious.

MAURICE

Shall we stay here long?

DOCTOR

To the chauffeur.

Shall we stay here long?

CHAUFFEUR

Angrily.

How do I know? About ten minutes I think. Please hold the light for me.

Hands the lantern to the doctor.

MAURICE

Then I will come out.

JEANNE

You had better stay here, Maurice. You may hurt your arm.

MAURICE

53

No, mother, I am careful. Where is the step? How inconvenient. Why don't they throw the flashlight here?

Jumps off and watches the chauffeur at work.

MAURICE

How unfortunate that we are stuck here!

CHAUFFEUR

Grumbling.

A bridge! How can anybody drive across such a bridge?

DOCTOR

Yes, it is unfortunate. We should have started out earlier.

MAURICE

Shrugging his shoulders.

Father did not want to leave. How could we start? Mamina, do you think our people are already in Antwerp?

JEANNE

Yes, I think so. Emil, aren't you cold?

EMIL GRELIEU

No. It is very pleasant to breathe the fresh air. I feel stronger.

DOCTOR

To Maurice.

I think we are still in the region which—

MAURICE

Yes. What time is it, Doctor?

DOCTOR

Looking at his watch.

Twenty—a quarter of ten.

MAURICE

Then it is a quarter of an hour since the bursting of the dams. Yes! Mamma, do you hear, it is a quarter of ten now!

JEANNE

Yes, I hear.

MAURICE

But it is strange that we haven't heard any explosions.

DOCTOR

How can you say that, Monsieur Maurice? It is very far away.

MAURICE

I thought that such explosions would be heard a hundred kilometers away. My God, how strange it is! Our house and our garden will soon be flooded! I wonder how high the water will rise. Do you think it will reach up to the second story?

DOCTOR

Possibly. Well, how are things moving?

CHAUFFEUR

Grumbling.

I am working.

MAURICE

Look, look! Mamma, see how the searchlights are working. They seem to be frightened. Father, do you see them?

EMIL GRELIEU

Jeanne, lift me a little.

JEANNE

My dear, I don't know whether I am allowed to do it.

DOCTOR

You may lift him a little, if it isn't very painful. The bandage is tight.

JEANNE

Do you feel any pain?

EMIL GRELIEU

No. They are frightened.

MAURICE

Father, they are flashing the searchlights across the sky like madmen. Look, look!

A bluish light is flashed over them, faintly illuminating the whole group.

MAURICE

Right into my eyes! Does that come from an elevation, father?

EMIL GRELIEU

I suppose so. Either they have been warned, or the water is reaching them by this time.

JEANNE

Do you think so, Emil?

EMIL GRELIEU

Yes. It seems to me that I hear the sound of the water from that side.

All listen and look in the direction from which the noise came.

DOCTOR

Uneasily.

How unpleasant this is! We should have started out sooner. We are too late.

MAURICE

Father, it seems to me I hear voices. Listen—it sounds as though they are crying there. Many, many people. Father, the Prussians are crying. It is they!

A distant, dull roaring of a crowd is heard. Then the crash of shots resounds. Sobs of military horns. The searchlights are swaying from side to side.

EMIL GRELIEU

It is they.

DOCTOR

If we don't start in a quarter of an hour—

EMIL GRELIEU

In half an hour, Doctor.

MAURICE

Father, how beautiful and how terrible it is! Give me your hand, mother.

JEANNE

What is it?

MAURICE

I want to kiss it. Mother, you have no gloves on!

JEANNE

What a foolish little boy you are, Maurice.

MAURICE

Monsieur Langloi said that in three days from now I may remove my bandage. Just think of it, in three days I shall be able to take up my gun again!... Oh, who is that? Look, who is that?

All near the automobile assume defensive positions. The chauffeur and the doctor draw their revolvers. A figure appears from the field, approaching from one of the ditches. A peasant, wounded in the leg, comes up slowly, leaning upon a cane.

MAURICE

Who is there?

PEASANT

Our own, our own. And who are you? Are you going to the city?

MAURICE

Yes, we're going to the city. Our car has broken down, we're repairing it. What are you doing here?

PEASANT

What am I doing here?

Examines the unfamiliar faces curiously. They also look at him attentively, by the light of the lantern.

CHAUFFEUR

Give me the light!

PEASANT

Are you carrying a wounded man? I am also wounded, in my leg. I cannot walk, it is very hard. I must lean on my cane. Are you going to the city? I lay there in the ditch and when I heard you speak French I crawled out. My name is Jaqular.

DOCTOR

How were you wounded?

PEASANT

I was walking in the field and they shot me. They must have thought I was a rabbit. Laughs hoarsely.

They must have thought I was a rabbit. What is the news, gentlemen? Is our Belgium lost?

Laughs.

Eh? Is our Belgium lost?

MAURICE

Don't you know?
PEASANT
What can I know? I lay there and looked at the sky—that's all I know. Did you see the sky? Just look at it, I have been watching it all the time. What is that I see in the sky, eh? How would you explain it?
EMIL GRELIEU
Sit down near us.
MAURICE

Listen, sit down here. It seems you haven't heard anything. You must get away from here. Do you know that the dams are broken? Do you understand? The dams!

PEASANT

The dams?

MAURICE

Yes. Don't you hear the cries over there? Listen! They are crying there—the Prussians!

PEASANT

Water?

MAURICE

Water. It must be reaching them now. They must have learned of it by this time. Listen, it is so far, and yet we can hear!

The peasant laughs hoarsely.

MAURICE

Sit down, right here, the automobile is large. Doctor, help him. I will hold the lantern.

CHAUFFEUR

Muttering.

Sit down, sit down! Eh!

DOCTOR

Uneasily.

What is it? Bad? Chauffeur, be quick! We can't stay here! The water is coming. We should have started out earlier.

MAURICE

What an unfortunate mishap!

JEANNE

Agitated.

They shot you like a rabbit? Do you hear, Emil—they thought a rabbit was running! Did you resemble a rabbit so closely?

She laughs loudly, the peasant also laughs.

PEASANT

I look like a rabbit! Exactly like a rabbit.

JEANNE

Do you hear, Emil? He says he looks exactly like a rabbit!

Laughs.

EMIL GRELIEU

Jeanne!

MAURICE

Mamma!

JEANNE

It makes me laugh—it seems so comical to me that they mistake us for rabbits. And now, what are we now—water rats? Emil, just picture to yourself, water rats in an automobile!

MAURICE

Mamma!

JEANNE

No, no, I am not laughing any more, Maurice!

Laughs.

And what else are we? Moles? Must we hide in the ground?

PEASANT

Laughs.

And now we must hide in the ground—

JEANNE

In the same tone.

And they will remain on the ground? Emil, do you hear?

EMIL GRELIEU

My dear! My dear!

MAURICE

To the doctor.

Listen, you must do something. Haven't you anything? Listen! Mamma, we are starting directly, my dear!

JEANNE

No, never mind, I am not laughing any more. How foolish you are. Maurice, I simply felt like talking. I was silent too long. I was forever silent, but just now I felt like chattering. Emil, I am not disturbing you with my talk, am I? Why is the water so quiet, Emil? It was the King who said, "The water is silent," was it not? But I should like to see it roar, crash like thunder.... No, I cannot, I cannot bear this silence! Ah, why is it so quiet—I cannot bear it!

MAURICE

To the chauffeur.

My dear fellow, please hurry up!

CHAUFFEUR

Yes, yes! I'm working, I'm working. We'll start soon.

JEANNE

Suddenly cries, threatening.

But I cannot bear it! I cannot!

Covers her mouth with her hands; sobs.

I cannot!

MAURICE

Mamma!

EMIL GRELIEU

All will end well, Jeanne. All will end well. I know. I also feel as you do. But all will end well, Jeanne!

JEANNE

Sobbing, but calming herself somewhat.

I cannot bear it!

EMIL GRELIEU

*All will end well, Jeanne! Belgium will live! The sun will shine! I am suffering, but_
know this, Jeanne!*

MAURICE

Quicker! Quicker!

CHAUFFEUR

In a moment, in a moment. Now it is fixed, in a moment.

EMIL GRELIEU

Faintly.

Jeanne!

JEANNE

Yes, yes, I know…. Forgive me, forgive me, I will soon—

A loud, somewhat hoarse voice of a girl comes from the dark.

GIRL

Tell me how I can find my way to Lonua!

Exclamations of surprise.

MAURICE

Who is that?

JEANNE

Emil, it is that girl!

Laughs.

She is also like a rabbit!

DOCTOR

Grumbles.

What is it, what is it—Who?

*Throws the light on the girl. Her dress is torn, her eyes look wild. The peasant is
laughing.*

PEASANT

She is here again?

CHAUFFEUR

Let me have the light!

DOCTOR

Very well!

GIRL

Loudly.

How can I find my way to Lonua?

EMIL GRELIEU

Maurice, you must stop her! My child, my child! Doctor, you—

CHAUFFEUR

Put down the lantern! The devil take this!

GIRL

Shouts.

Hands off! No, no, you will not dare—

MAURICE

You can't catch her—

The girl runs away.

EMIL GRELIEU

Doctor, you must catch her! She will perish here, quick—

She runs away. The doctor follows her in the dark.

PEASANT

She asked me, too, how to go to Lonua. How am I to know? Lonua!

The girl's voice resounds in the dark and then there is silence.

EMIL GRELIEU

You must catch her! What is it? You must!

MAURICE

But how, father?

They listen. Silence. Dull cries of a mob resound. Jeanne breaks into muffled laughter.

MAURICE

Mutters.

Now he is gone! Oh, my God!

CHAUFFEUR

Triumphantly.

Take your seats! Ready!

MAURICE

But the doctor isn't here. Oh, my God! Father, what shall we do now?

CHAUFFEUR

Let us call him. Eh!

Maurice and the chauffeur call: "Doctor! Eh! Langloi!"

CHAUFFEUR

Angrily.

I must deliver Monsieur Grelieu, and I will deliver him. Take your seats!

MAURICE

Shouts.

Langloi!

A faint echo in the distance.

Come! Doctor!

The response is nearer.

PEASANT

He did not catch her. You cannot catch her. She asked me, too, about the road to Lonua. She is insane.

Laughs.

There are many like her now.

EMIL GRELIEU

61

Imploringly.

Jeanne!

JEANNE

But I cannot, Emil. What is it? I cannot understand. What is it? Where are we? My God, I don't understand anything. I used to understand, I used to understand, but now—Where is Pierre? Firmly.

Where is Pierre?

MAURICE

Oh, will he be here soon? Mother dear, we'll start in a moment!

JEANNE

Yes, yes, we'll start in a moment! But I don't understand anything. Where are we? Why such a dream, why such a dream? I can't understand! Who has come? My head is aching. Who has come? Why has it happened?

A mice from the darkness, quite near.

JEANNE

Frightened.

Who is shouting? What a strange dream, what a terrible, terrible, terrible dream. Where is Pierre?

MAURICE

Mother!

JEANNE

I cannot!

Lowering her voice.

I cannot—why are you torturing me? Where is Pierre?

EMIL GRELIEU

He is dead, Jeanne!

JEANNE

No!!!

EMIL GRELIEU

He is dead, Jeanne. But I swear to you by God, Jeanne!—Belgium will live. Weep, sob, you are a mother. I too am crying with you—But I swear by God: Belgium will live! God has given me the light to see, and I can see. Songs will resound here. Jeanne! A new Spring will come here, the trees will be covered with blossoms—I swear to you, Jeanne, they will be covered with blossoms! And mothers will caress their children, and the sun will shine upon their heads, upon their golden-haired little heads! Jeanne! There will be no more bloodshed. I see a new world, Jeanne! I see my nation: Here it is advancing with palm leaves to meet God who has come to earth again. Weep, Jeanne, you are a mother! Weep, unfortunate mother—God weeps with you. But there will be happy mothers here again—I see a new world, Jeanne, I see a new life!

Curtain

DATE: ....

 **Notes**

 DATE: ....

Notes

DATE: ....

DATE:

 **Notes**

DATE: ....

 **Notes**

DATE: ....

 **Notes**

DATE: ....

....
....
....
....
....
....
....
....
....
....
....
....
....
....
....
....
....
....
....
....
....
....
....
....
....
....
....
....
....
....
....
....
....

Notes

Notes

DATE: ....

Notes

DATE: ....

DATE: ....

 Notes

DATE: ....

 **Notes**

DATE: ....

....
....
....
....
....
....
....
....
....
....
....
....
....
....
....
....
....
....
....
....
....
....
....
....
....
....
....
....
....
....

DATE: ....

DATE: ....

 Notes

Notes

DATE: ....